MARSHA + LARRY,

ALL MY BEST,

[signature]

CARRY OUT

JON BONNELL

CARRY ON

A YEAR
IN THE LIFE OF
A TEXAS CHEF

THE PANDEMIC OF
2020

© 2021 Jon Bonnell

ISBN: 978-1-09839-241-3

Editing by Kathy Harris
Book design by Cynthia Wahl

Scott Berkman

James Carver

Omar Escobar

Anthony Felli

Chad 'Sad Chad' Harkins

Kelcey Harris

Jamie Holderby

Lilia Islas

Spencer Marks

Felipe Melendez

Candice Miller

Alicia Rampey

Koby Rogers

James Pallett

This book is dedicated
to the team members who
helped steer our fine dining
restaurants through the
toughest of times.

Isela Salinas

Christen Withers

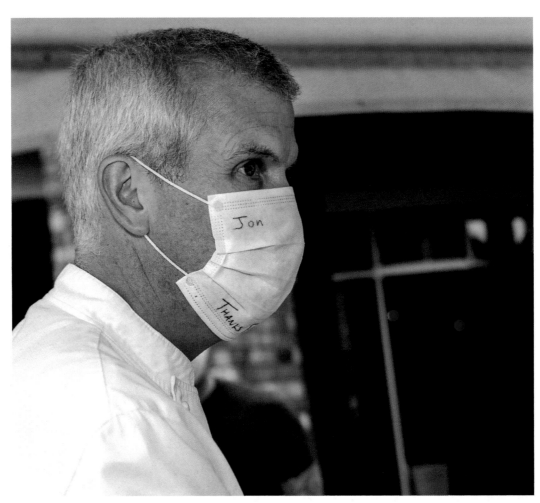

Photo by Walt Burns

FOREWORD

Jon Bonnell is a Fort Worth native and lifelong resident, a classically trained chef, and has been an independent restaurant owner for the past 20 years in the great city of Fort Worth. With four restaurant locations in this city and a deep sense of pride in his hometown, he was a natural choice when I needed to relay valuable information to our local business owners and independent operators during the COVID-19 pandemic.

In one year, my office had more changes and updates passing through than in the three years prior all added together, making efficiency a top priority when disseminating critical communications to our community. Jon helped us get out every detail of information to the Fort Worth business community and spoke at critical meetings and press conferences.

Demonstrating his dedication to the well-being of his fellow chefs and restaurateurs, he even took the task one step further by creating a support network for all the independent restaurant owners in the area. His email list grew quickly as he informed the community of new regulations, restrictions, critical health data, and even helped with vital PPP loan and local grant information. He became the communication hub between the community and me, Tarrant County Judge Glen Whitley, Gov. Greg Abbott, and even Sen. John Cornyn during a time when the business landscape was changing every day.

He led by example with an innovative spirit as his businesses' takeout family meals served curbside became the model for many other establishments, helping feed a desperate community at the same time.

His unwavering support of others helped steer countless mom & pop operators through troubled times, resulting in many beloved Fort Worth restaurants being able to survive the year. During times of fear and uncertainty, Jon stepped up as a trusted leader and friend to all of Fort Worth.

— Betsy Price, Fort Worth Mayor (2011-2021)

Photo by Walt Burns

February 2020 | All Is Well

The month of February 2020 marked the last time that my world felt "*normal*." That word has been thrown around haphazardly for over a year now. "When do we get back to *normal*?"; "Is this the new *normal*?"; "When is it safe to just act *normal* again?"

So many great life events occurred in February that I could not have imagined what was on the horizon. My best friend and I took a bucket-list fly-fishing trip for my 50th birthday to New Zealand, and I landed the fish of a lifetime, a 30-inch, 10-pound brown trout on a fly rod! My usual group of friends took our annual pilgrimage to Mardi Gras and had an amazing experience, with fantastic food and the famous party scene, riding with the Krewe of Bacchus and tossing beads to screaming bystanders until my arm was sore.

I came home exhausted from a typical Louisiana weekend but didn't have time to rest. This was the beginning of the busy season for a chef. I had a bit of a sinus infection, but with so much on the calendar, I just took some Advil and went to work — no time to slow down.

Shortly after we returned, my 12-year-old daughter, Charlotte, came on her first official catering gig with me at a private event, donning an official chef's jacket and everything. She earned her keep, constructing and decorating immaculate appetizer platters, and she was enthralled by the idea of hanging out with the band in the

Trout of a lifetime in New Zealand!

Catering with my daughter!

"So many great life events occurred in February that I could not have imagined what was on the horizon."

Working the Cowtown Marathon, and congratulating Ernie Lacroix on his finish.

kitchen for a while before they entertained the crowd. The catering schedule was jam-packed throughout February, and I was bouncing all over town during one the busiest seasons I can remember. The Sportsmen's Club Banquet went off without a hitch (over 1,000 attendees) on the last Thursday of the month, then the Cowtown Marathon had its 41st running with almost 20,000 participants. I was on the microphone, calling out the names of finishers, including Ernie Lacroix, who celebrated his 100th birthday by running the 5K with his family. I got the crowd involved by singing "Happy Birthday" to Ernie as he approached the home stretch, then made my way through the sweaty pack of finishers just to shake his hand and congratulate the man. What an accomplishment!

8

March Madness

The first week of March began with very little fanfare, although the national news had just started mentioning the arrival of some new kind of virus that we all needed to understand. We had already lived through swine flu, Asian bird flu, SARS, and this just seemed to fall right in line with virus strains that we had already been through and survived. It barely even grabbed our attention, aside from the great memes that we began circulating among friends. "If you ever ate dinner at Pancho's Buffet, you are likely immune to the Corona virus." "If you ever drank trash can punch in college, your body is fully immune to The Rona."

As the news stations continued to share stories of this new virus and its toll on places in Europe, our antennae went up a bit and we listened more attentively. My daughter's spring break trip got canceled, so without any plans for the week, my wife and I opted to head down to Rough Creek Lodge in Glen Rose for a little staycation with our two kids, hoping things would all just pass quietly. Officials at our kids' school had them bring home all of their books as a precaution in case students needed to take more than a week of vacation. We caught a few fish, did a little target shooting, played on zip lines, threw tomahawks, and dined on some fabulous

Texas cuisine from Chef Gerard Thompson.

While talking with Gerard, he expressed some concern about how many of their reservations were getting canceled. My wife noticed that my energy level wasn't quite what it should be, as I took a nap almost every afternoon, which was not normal behavior for me. Maybe this low-key staycation was just the kind of rest and recharge that I needed.

By the second week of March, all four of our restaurants — Bonnell's, Waters and two Buffalo Bros locations — were in total chaos. This virus, now referred to by its more formal name, COVID-19, was dominating every single news cycle. Sales in all of our restaurants were down 90%. By calling and texting everyone else I knew in the industry, I quickly learned that we were not alone. Every restaurant in the area was bleeding money — profusely. Without cash flow, very few restaurants can last more than a few months. People were scared. Customers lit up the phone lines with cancellations. We could watch an entirely full night of reservations just melt away in a matter of hours.

On March 14, we had a meeting with the employees of Bonnell's Restaurant in Fort Worth and decided to drastically cut our hours of operation and our number of staff. We announced that lunch service would cease, allowing us to focus on just dinner and try to ride this storm out until sales came back. Our catering department was set to

"How in the hell are we going to run a sports bar on a college campus with no sports and no college?"

have a record-setting year with formal parties, graduations, weddings, etc.; we were packed to the gills on our 2020 calendar. In a matter of four days, the events disappeared — the calendar was wiped completely clean. Hundreds of thousands of dollars in contracted sales for the year just vanished into the wind.

It didn't feel right to keep deposits on these contracts, so we quickly depleted our account as the money flowed out. As I sat next to my business partner, Ed McOwen, at one of our bars, we watched

The only March madness Buffalo Bros saw was empty seats and expiring beer kegs.

in horror as the NBA announced the cancellation of its entire season. Schools were closed, more events were canceled, the entire economy was in a tailspin with no end in sight. I looked at Ed and asked, "How in the hell are we going to run a sports bar on a college campus with no sports and no college?" All of our money was tied up in these restaurants, our livelihoods and savings just being flushed away. Our newest sports bar

had just opened in August, complete with 93 flat-screen TVs and 72 beers on tap. It wasn't cheap, it wasn't paid for, and it wasn't going to make a dime during what should have been the March Madness basketball tournament in the NCAA. Instead, our entire society was facing a different kind of "March Madness" altogether.

March 12 | The Meeting

The Fort Worth Food + Wine Festival had a clay shoot fundraiser scheduled for Monday, March 16, at my family's ranch just west of the city. On Thursday the week prior, we reluctantly made the call to cancel the event completely, even though it was sold out. I asked some of the other restaurateurs, business owners, and chefs if they still wanted to get together at the ranch and just talk about what was going on. When Mayor Betsy Price agreed to attend, everyone followed suit. About 15 of us gathered in the largest room in the house and spaced our chairs 6 feet apart, the first time any of us had heard of or practiced this new term: "social distancing." I asked my brother Ric to join, since he's a global health expert, physician and professor of medicine.

We began the meeting with introductions, then all eyes focused on Ric as the question was asked: "What's really going on? Is this as bad as the news is saying?" "In a short answer, yes," Ric replied. "Let me read you all some of the medical data from countries in Europe." As he laid out the numbers of cases and deaths being reported by European countries, we all suddenly felt the weight of the situation.

Mayor Price told us in no uncertain terms, "I have no intention of shutting down the restaurants of Fort Worth." Within 2 minutes of her statement, another restaurant owner held up his iPhone and announced, "Dallas just shut down all of their restaurants. Yup, all of 'em." The room went silent for quite some time, and the gravity of the situation hit everyone like a ton of bricks. We all knew what was about to happen, and we knew it wouldn't be long.

Mayor Price asked us to get organized and designate a point person to handle all official information coming from her office. It made perfect sense. I was amazed that she could find the time to meet with us in the first place. Her phone blew up the entire meeting, but to her credit, she stayed and answered all of our questions. That's just the kind of mayor she was, never hiding from her city or its citizens. As it turned out, that point person became me. I was given the email list from the Food + Wine Festival as a great starting place for relaying official information as it became available, and I've been expanding the list ever since.

I couldn't sleep that night, so I made myself busy copying the entire email list into an organized group that I could easily use on my laptop. The format didn't translate from its Microsoft version to my Apple version, so I just retyped each email address. What else did I have to do all night? I then scoured all of my contacts to add anyone else who might need information as well.

"What's really going on? Is this as bad as the news is saying?" "In a short answer, yes."

Email Correspondence – Critical Communication Begins

March 12

Hello friends and colleagues,

A group of independent restaurant owners, Chefs, and small business owners met today with Mayor Price, the Health Secretary of Ft Worth and medical professionals. I know you are all suffering. We all need to stick together, pray, and help each other through these difficult times. Here are a few of the bullet points that we discussed.

1. This pandemic is bigger and worse than initially realized, and the numbers of sick and infected will likely skyrocket this week as test kits come back.

2. Dallas has closed restaurant and bar traffic, but Ft Worth has not and has no plans as of now to do so.

3. Social distancing is a must for everyone.

4. Fine dining is a concept that might just need to be put to bed until we see the other side of this thing. The public doesn't exactly need crab legs and Kobe right now.

5. Restaurants and stores have an obligation to socially distance people who show up. Seat tables as far away as possible. Limit the number and proximity of barstools.

6. Loss of business insurance is unlikely to cover any of this, but different policies vary.

7. Anyone who appears or feels sick in any way should not be at a restaurant in any capacity for any reason, employee or customer. The most important symptoms to look for are sore throat, cough, sniffles, fever. The hardest part of containing this virus is knowing that a person can be contagious for days before showing signs of sickness.

8. All restaurants and businesses are in exactly the same situation as you are right now. You are not alone.

9. Several states and cities have required the closure of all restaurants and bars. This is likely going to happen here at some point. We do not have any timeline of when this might occur, but the outlook does remain likely. The Mayor's office is getting pressure to do this, but for now is resisting. If the Governor or President calls for it, we are all shut down.

10. The CDC has recommended that no more than 50 people be in a place together. This is not law, only suggested and was intended to be for public gatherings.

11. Many states and cities have already closed restaurants and bars. We might have no choice soon. See the link for a current list https://www.foxnews.com/food-drink/states-closing-bars-restaurants-coronavirus-outbreak

12. Visit Fort Worth has agreed to build us a website that can help put all information about what each restaurant is doing in one simple format. We can all take advantage of that soon.

I just got off the phone with the Mayor a few minutes ago. We are going to use this as a portal of communication from the restaurants to the Mayor's office. Please do not hit the "reply all" button for every question. This list is almost 100 strong and I will do my best to answer questions as they come up, but I'm just one dude, so please be patient. I'm attaching the latest from the Mayor's office below in a PDF. If you have medical questions, I can do my best to answer as well. My brother is a global health expert, a Physician, ER doctor and professor at the TCU med school. Again, please be sparing with what you have. I'm just the hub here.

Speaking on behalf of Bonnell's, we are likely to keep serving on a very limited basis this week in our fine dining restaurants, then attempt to move to a family meal pricing model of food for pickup next week, closing the dining rooms. We have cut a very large amount of our labor. Our casual Buffalo Bros restaurants will likely drastically reduce in house dining and attempt to move towards curbside and delivery as much as possible. Many in attendance today are likely to just close until the storm blows over. I wish I had some better news to share right now, but we all have more questions than answers. Stay safe, my friends. I hope we can all come through this crisis and celebrate one day on the other side. See below for the latest from Betsy.

Jon Bonnell

March 17 | **Close Your Doors**

On the morning of Tuesday, March 17, we all got the call that we knew was inevitable, but it was still a shock nonetheless. All restaurants in the city of Fort Worth must close by midnight Wednesday until further notice. I was asked to help represent independent restaurants at the Tarrant County Courthouse that afternoon. After Mayor Price and Tarrant County Judge Glen Whitley made their remarks, I made an impassioned plea to the people of Fort Worth on live television. "Please keep supporting your local establishments as much as you can. They will not get through this crisis without you." As I spoke the words, I fought back tears as it suddenly hit me like a ton of bricks that many of my friends and colleagues in the industry weren't going to survive this pandemic. Our industry would never again be the same.

I sent out my second email newsletter to the group and asked everyone to send me any contacts whom I might have missed.

March 17
From Mayor Price,

All restaurants and bars are to close their dining rooms in the next 24 hours. The timeline has been set for midnight tomorrow. Please plan on switching to a pickup, curbside, or delivery option by tomorrow night.

Sending out a virtual hug to each and every one of you. Please try to stay strong and stay safe out there. We are all in this together.

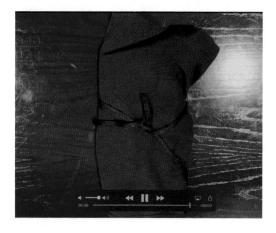

Scan this QR Code, like we do in restaurants now, to view Taps being played for the waitperson.

"Please keep supporting your local establishments as much as you can. They will not get through this crisis without you."

Sundance Square, in downtown Fort Worth, became a ghost town

March 17 | **Shutting Down**

After the announcement from the mayor on March 17, I scheduled an all-employee meeting on the patio of Waters Restaurant in Sundance Square. Everyone had heard rumors about the mayor's order but desperately needed to hear from me what the actual plan was going to be. We had never gathered all the employees of the restaurant in one place. There is a lunch crew that starts very early in the morning, and a dinner crew that works very late into the night, but they had never all been together in one place and time, until now.

I tried to rehearse this speech in my head a hundred times on the drive over. I parked several blocks away in front of our sports bar, Buffalo Bros, so that I would have a chance to walk and clear my head one last time before facing everyone. It was a beautiful, sunny spring morning, but usually-bustling downtown Fort Worth had been replaced by a ghost town, not a car on the street.

Every single employee of Waters was standing on the patio as I rounded the corner, and the silence became deafening as I climbed up the front stairs. "Good morning, everyone (biggest lie ever). The mayor has ordered us to close our doors. We don't have any choice. I have to let you go. You all deserve better, and I wish I had another option, but we are now closed and there's nothing else we can do. The only advice I can give you all is to get on the unemployment website and keep trying, keep calling until you get registered. Millions of people will be on the system today, and it will likely crash. Just keep trying. Please stay safe. I love you all and hope I can hire you all back very soon."

And with that there were tears, hugs, emotional promises and then, finally, just the slow shuffle of everyone leaving, many for the last time as colleagues as we concluded our very first all-staff meeting. How ironic. The job titles of waiter/waitress, host/hostess, wine steward and bartender no longer existed in our city. An entire service industry, a community that I dearly loved and worked as a part of for over 20 years, just vanished in the blink of an eye.

We ended up keeping only six employees at Waters, trying desperately to hold onto something. Curbside service was our only option, so I kept four kitchen staff and two managers, then started working on a plan. That was the most emotionally draining morning I can remember, as I fired so many people who had done nothing wrong. Nobody was blaming me, but I still felt the immense guilt and helplessness of just letting everyone go. That was only the first of four such meetings on March 17 — one at each restaurant. All told, we fired 234 people by that evening, leaving only 31 employees to run (or attempt to run) all the Bonnell's establishments.

Just to put an extra sharp point on the day, when I finally drove away from my spot in front of Buffalo Bros, I found a parking ticket on my car, even though my car was the only one parked for blocks around. I guess the meter readers were still considered "essential employees." I had forgotten to display my official parking permit from the rearview mirror when I parked that morning. I guess my mind must have been focused on something else. Looked like I'd be adding "contest my ticket" to the list of things to do that day. I ended up losing that fight, and had to pay the fine after all.

What Now? Curbside Dining?

The afternoon of March 18, I called a meeting with the few staff members whom I had left. The Buffalo Bros locations cut plenty of staff, but they could still operate with the same menu as before. It wasn't as difficult to serve pizza, wings and subs from the curbside and/or by delivery services, since that type of food is pretty well-suited to takeout already. But what about the two fine dining restaurants? How in the world were we going to save these two upscale, full-service, white-tablecloth establishments with only six people?

As I started the meeting at our original Bonnell's location, we all stayed at least 6 feet apart. I began by stating, "The bar is open, so please just help yourself. I know for damn sure that I need a drink!" I sat down and drank with the managers and chefs who were left, not many in number but all very essential partners in our businesses. Several pulled me aside and asked if they were really even needed, likely feeling a form of survivor's guilt for still being employed in 2020. "All ideas are on the table here, guys. What can we do to survive this?" I asked. We poured over everything we could think of. We discussed just serving our regular menu to-go. "What if we just pay ex-servers cash to deliver everything?"

We discussed changing our current menu to more casual, to-go-friendly options and hiring a delivery service. We even discussed just closing until the virus was over. The hardest part of this discussion boiled down to my inevitable conclusion that our entire restaurant concept was no longer relevant in this time of crisis. Fine dining no longer had a place, no more meaning. It felt shallow to even try to hold onto something so based on indulgence from its inception.

I've been a chef for most of my life, thinking about dishes, ingredients, presentations, new and unique flavors. What did any of that even matter anymore? The people of Fort Worth didn't need exotic ingredients or oysters on the half-shell. The people needed to eat. In this crisis, our first step needed to be a complete abandonment of our brands, our menus, our entire concepts. I felt almost a sense of shame for being in the fine dining industry for so many years. The entire endeavor now felt hollow. There was no way to offer our regular type of cuisine in plastic bags at the curbside, so we simply abandoned the fine dining mantra altogether.

I finally put into words the framework that I'd been contemplating in my head. "What if we just begin with this principal: Feed the most people possible, for the least amount of money we can afford? Let's start with family meals, $40 a bag feeds the whole family."

My staff (what was left of them) thought I was crazy. Hell, they were probably right, but what other viable options did we have? "You want us to make hundreds of meals, all exactly the same, wrap them up in bags, and serve everyone outside with no options? So, we're not even going to take orders?" they asked. "Yep, that's pretty much it," I replied. "We need to feed the most, for what costs the least. We couldn't take individual orders even if we wanted to. We don't have any staff left to answer the phones."

"I've been a chef for most of my life, thinking about dishes, ingredients, presentations, new and unique flavors. What did any of that even matter anymore?"

The popularity of curbside pickup was immediate.

Getting Critical Information Distributed – By Email

With an ever-changing landscape of rules, regulations and rapidly evolving policy changes, the email correspondence list became a crucial method of distributing information.

March 17 1:36pm

Hello all,

I hope everyone is staying safe and in good spirits, at least as good as can be expected. I have word from the Mayor's office that we are likely to have dining rooms and bars shutdown sometime soon. She has not declared anything yet, but it is her belief that this announcement may come as early as Wednesday or Thursday, so be prepared.

Most restaurants are choosing one of 2 paths moving forward: Close and terminate employees, or move to a delivery, curbside delivery, no-contact option.

I can tell you that we are converting Bonnell's and Waters to curbside only, starting on Saturday. $40 meals for 4 people, family style, inexpensive. I think fine dining is a concept we may need to dismiss for a while. As grocery stores get more pressure, there will be a need to provide home meal replacement and that is the direction that we are taking. Buffalo Bros is more able to adapt to takeout and delivery systems that are already in place. I wish I had better news to share, my friends but I do not. I have let 90% of my staff go. Let's all pray together that this passes by and we can all hit the reset button. The medical news is likely to get worse before it gets better, so be prepared. 2 new community cases have been reported this morning. I love this community as much as you do, so let's all try to keep everyone safe and fed. FYI, the food bank and all grocery stores have said they are hiring people on a "paid volunteer" type of basis, but I have not researched exactly what that entails.

I will continue to keep you all up to speed as official information becomes available.

Jon Bonnell

March 17, 5:43pm

Here is the latest news from the City.

Everyone is being issued the strong suggestion that we need to be preparing for a shutdown of all dining rooms and bars in the next 24 hours. This has not been mandated, but is being suggested for us to prepare. We are all being advised to move to a model of curbside pickup or delivery. I'm guessing that we will be officially mandated to shut down on Thursday, or maybe even as early as tomorrow night.

Mitch Whitten from Visit Fort Worth has set up a website for us to utilize that clearly states exactly what each and every restaurant is offering. I encourage everyone to use this website as a clear and consolidated list of restaurants in Ft Worth. We are much stronger together, all sending out the same link to this website than any of us can be alone. If you plan on closing, and I know a lot of you are, please advise the website so that it can be kept up to date. To be included, or removed from this website, please see below. It is being done at zero cost. I encourage everyone to utilize this site, then use the power of your email lists and social media to all get out this same link. Let's get a united and consolidated message to the public. We will all be safer moving to a contact-free curbside meal service or delivery service by utilizing this method. No judgment for those who need to shut down, but please update the site to reflect it.

Still sending prayers and best wishes for all of you, your families, friends, and your staff. I let 90% of my people go today, and I know many of you have taken similar steps. We are switching to curbside only, beginning Saturday. Take care my friends. I will keep you all posted as I find out any new information.

Jon Bonnell

Visit Fort Worth has launched a new website listing restaurants doing take-out and will promote this heavily. You can add your information by emailing AustinJames@FortWorth.com.
No cost to restaurants.
https://www.fortworth.com/coronavirus/restaurant-updates/

March 18
From Mayor Price

All restaurants and bars are to close their dining rooms in the next 24 hours. The timeline has been set for midnight tomorrow. Please plan on switching to a pickup, curbside, or delivery option by tomorrow night.

Sending out a virtual hug to each and every one of you. Please try to stay strong and stay safe out there. We are all in this together.

March 18

Hello all,

I just finished up a press conference with Mayor Price, County Judge Glen Whitley, and the Mayors of Kennedale, Grand Prairie, & North Richland Hills. Here are a few of my notes to pass along. As of Midnight tonight, all bars, restaurants, dining rooms, amusement centers, gyms, bingo halls, and private country clubs are shut down. If you own a restaurant or bar, no patrons are allowed inside. You can produce food and sell curbside or deliver, but customers may not enter the building. All other places are limited to gatherings of no more than 50 ppl, public or private. The city has made this mandatory, the County is strongly urging it. It's hard to govern, since the County has 41 different cities, but they plan strict enforcement throughout the County. Public Health department has had to do zero enforcement so far, only because of the complete cooperation from people like you. Please use the comprehensive website that was given by visitfw.com to list which places are still open and what you might be offering.

One other takeaway from this meeting: All city services such as electric, water, gas, etc will not be interrupted and not be disconnected for non-payment. This might really be good to tell your employees that may have been let go. Their services will not be disconnected if they do not pay. They might just defer the payment, but for now, no disconnections allowed. The city will also not allow any evictions for nonpayment at this time. Please pass this on.

Tim Love has closed all of his restaurants, but has concentrated some of his kitchen staff at his catering kitchen. He plans to provide free meals for anyone who needs it, lunch from 12-2, dinner from 3-5 hot meals for anyone, just show up. 713 Main, kitchen door around back. If you have employees who really need it, please let them know about this.

Hang in there, everyone. Love you all. Stay safe.

Jon Bonnell

Getting Critical Information Distributed – By Email

March 18, 8:30pm
*This is an extremely positive step! Yesssssssssss!!!
Governor Abbott announced that he will lift all restrictions
pertaining to alcohol sales from restaurants. Bottom line,
we can now sell alcohol to go!*

March 19
*I have gotten a lot of questions from y'all about alcohol.
Ken Paxton did say "mixed beverages" on the radio. The
actual language coming from our TRA leader and attorney
is below. It does not allow mixing beverages. Beer, wine,
spirits (375s) and things like White Claw are all good to go
for sure. Mixing is your own judgement call. I doubt there's
much enforcement, but this is the print version here.*

*Please know that there is a very good chance we could be
in complete lockdown within a week or 2. It is not clear in
any way what that would mean to restaurants.*

March 19
*With monthly taxes due tomorrow, Craig Goldman (state
rep) reached out to the Comptroller personally to try and
get some tax relief. Not much love in the response, but
here's the official answer from the Comptroller.*

*"The business needs to file their tax paperwork and call our
enforcement hotline if they want to enter into a payment
plan if they cannot pay in full. Number is 800-252-8880"*

March 19
*Governor Abbott has officially shut down all restaurants and
bars in the state. No more city by city, county by county. To
go, curbside, and delivery only. Solid move.*

Governor Abbott Waives Certain Regulations To Allow Delivery Of Alcohol From Restaurants And To Support Hospitality Industry

GOVERNOR GREG ABBOTT

For Immediate Distribution | March 18, 2020 | (512) 463-1826

Governor Abbott Waives Certain Regulations To Allow Delivery Of Alcohol From Restaurants And To Support Hospitality Industry

AUSTIN - Governor Greg Abbott today issued a waiver that will allow restaurants to deliver alcoholic beverages with food purchases to patrons, including beer, wine, and mixed drinks. The Governor also directed the Texas Alcoholic Beverage Commission (TABC) to waive certain provisions to allow manufacturers, wholesalers, and retailers of alcoholic beverages to repurchase or sell back unopened product.

These waivers are in response to the financial hardship caused by COVID-19 that has disproportionately affected the hospitality industry.

"The State of Texas is committed to supporting retailers, restaurants, and their employees," said Governor Abbott. "These waivers will allow restaurants to provide enhanced delivery options to consumers during this temporary period of social distancing."

Under this waiver, effective immediately, restaurants with a mixed beverage permit may sell beer, wine, or mixed drinks for delivery as long as they are accompanied by food purchased from the restaurant.

The buy-back waiver allows alcohol distributors and manufacturers to repurchase excess inventory from restaurants, bars, and clubs affected by event cancellations due to COVID-19.

###

"Just cook as many meal kits as we can, and I'll try to sell them."

Late March | Setting the Stage

This was uncharted territory to say the least. We turned off all of our phone lines and left a recording with simple instructions about our new family meal offering. Our entire elaborately-designed websites were replaced with a basic splash page sharing our very simple plan. Bonnell's and Waters would offer four-person family meals for $40 — no substitutions, no choices, no pre-orders, just show up and grab one, starting on Saturday, the 21st of March. I rented a huge neon-colored sign to advertise our meals to the traffic passing by. Fortunately, a few days before our first curbside service, the governor of Texas had thrown out a huge lifeline! He took away all restrictions about serving alcohol, allowing us to sell booze at the curb. He also lifted restrictions on the selling of groceries, so we could sell every single item in our inventory as we started this new type of service.

I decided to utilize the only free method of advertising at my disposal. Social media became the best communication tool I had, and I spread the word on our menu feature each morning on Facebook. "Just cook as many meal kits as we can, and I'll try to sell them," I told the staff. Only four people worked in the kitchen at Bonnell's, and another four at Waters, while just two staff members were left to run the curbside at

In our haste to get this sign up, we had a glaring typo. Normally an unforgivable error, this really wasn't the biggest problem we were facing. It didn't even make the top 10!

each location. That was it. We had no idea of how much food to prepare. Would anyone even show up? Would everyone show up and overwhelm us? There was no way to even guess how this would work, or if this would work. There was no "expert" in the field I could contact and ask for advice. Everyone was flying blind this time. We cooked, packed bags, and braced for the unknown.

March 21 | Day 1 on the Curb

The first service was scheduled to begin at 4 p.m. on Saturday, March 21. I had advertised the meals of the evening on my Facebook page, then shared them accordingly to the Waters page and the Bonnell's page. Brisket, sausage, mac 'n' cheese, slaw, biscuits, salad, and cookies. Waters started with king salmon (utilizing what we still had in-house), scallops, Caesar salad, garlic bread, asparagus, and pasta. The Bonnell's meals came refrigerated with simple heating instructions, while we served hot seafood at Waters.

I thought some people might show up a little early, so at 3:30 I walked outside the front doors with Kelcey (our catering director) and we were instantly overwhelmed by the terrifying scene laid out before us. Cars were jammed into the Bonnell's parking lot, all facing each other, coming in from every single direction. Total gridlock and confusion. I wanted to cry and just quit right there, but it was too late. We had committed to this plan; now we had to make good on our promises.

We used a wireless credit card reader from Square to take payments, put on gloves and masks, sanitized every surface and just dove right into the chaos. We served the last guy in line first so that he could back up his truck into the street and leave, then proceeded to serve the rest of the cars in this fashion, allowing each one to back out. Then we served the cars that were parked in actual spaces, although they were still pretty much blocked in and wouldn't be able to leave for a while. Just as it felt like we

might have a chance at this thing, we suddenly ran out of food and had to disappoint an alarming number of customers.

I went online to make a massive public apology, but people were remarkably understanding and supportive of our efforts. It was time to regroup and come up with a better plan for the next day. That evening, once again, the bar was simply open to all employees — those who were left anyway. We had a few drinks and discussed what went wrong and how to fix it. The kitchen didn't have trouble with the volume of food needed, but packaging everything up became the toughest obstacle. If we served 125 meal kits, that meant 125 containers of meat, 125 containers of salad, 125 containers of mac 'n' cheese, etc. With just four sets of hands, the packaging itself was more cumbersome than actually cooking the food, and our suppliers were having a hard time stocking enough containers, as every restaurant in town was now switching from in-house service to takeout only.

"I wanted to cry and just quit."

Photo by Walt Burns

Our private banquet room was transformed into the "packaging room."

March 21

Kelcey and I came up with a much better plan for traffic for the next day. Cars would all need to go in the same direction, enter from the frontage road, then exit the other side. Luckily, our parking lot was equipped with multiple entrances and exits, but we needed to get more organized to control the flow of traffic. The good news was that we were busy and customers showed up. The bad news was that so many customers showed up that we had to disappoint hundreds of people.

When we finally counted the money for the evening, I assumed there must have been a huge mistake. The sales were pretty much what I thought they'd be, based on how much food we made, but we had massive amounts of cash. The tips were more than I could have ever imagined! The generosity of people was truly overwhelming. I decided to tip everyone still on staff $100 each and start putting the rest of the tip money into a fund. We could figure out later how to use it, but for now we had more pressing issues to deal with. We called it a night, cleaned up and planned to come in early the next day. Waters Restaurant didn't have a parking lot, so its line just wrapped around the streets of Sundance Square. Waters sold out quickly as well, but with far less confusion and chaos.

March 22 | Day 2 on the Curb

I started the day by ordering in lunch from another independent restaurant for the staff. Everyone could use the extra business, and we wanted to support locally owned places as often as possible. We strategically parked employee cars to block off all entrances to the parking lot other than the one on the frontage road. A good friend brought us traffic cones from his business and had signs printed up for the exit and entrance. He even made some great slogans for us, like "Please be patient! This is our first pandemic too!" We set

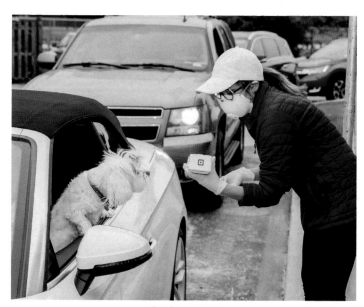

Photo by Walt Burns

25

Partnering with MELT Ice Creams turned out to be a great sales move for both of our businesses.

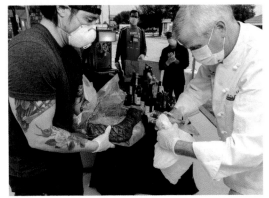

Photo by Walt Burns

March 22

up a table with various types of alcohol to sell, then added some extras from inventory like vacuum-packed steaks and fresh fish to the day's offering, kept inside a cooler I brought from my house. I rented a frozen margarita machine as well. I called a friend who owns a local ice cream shop, and she delivered a freezer and a few hundred pints of various MELT flavors for us to sell. Adding on to those $40 meals with steaks, ice cream, alcohol — whatever we could manage to sell — would be the fastest way to see any real profit. We needed to sell everything we had in our inventory as well.

Using Facebook once again, I gave instructions for traffic patterns as I laid

Our meal line was long, while the freeway traffic was almost nonexistent. Scan the QR Code below to see the drone footage.

out the menu for our second day of curbside service. Cars began to line up almost 2½ hours before our scheduled opening. I couldn't believe how fast the word had spread about our meals. Many customers didn't have any plans for the day, other than picking up a family meal, so hanging out in their car for the afternoon was as exciting as the day was going to get. Once we got started, service was smooth as silk. This was

Drone footage by Jack Bonnell

"Sad Chad" about to make his march up the line.

March 22

organized 100% better than the previous night. Our plan had worked, and we sold out in about two hours.

Once we got down to 50 meals, I sent our manager up the street to count cars and show everyone in line which car would be the last one we had enough food to serve. We lovingly referred to that manager as "Sad Chad." At least they didn't have to wait any longer, just to be disappointed.

Jon Bonnell
April 11, 2020 · 🌐 ···

For everyone who has waited in line, but missed the meals, MY MOST SINCERE APOLOGIES! We are trying to crank out as much food as we possibly can from our little kitchen with limited staff. Right now, our capacity is about 500 meals (125 kits) per day. The line has been forming a little before 3:00, and we start serving at 4:00. Most days, we serve the last car about 5:20. When we get down to 50 bags, I send a guy waaaaayyy up the hill to count cars and let anyone past the 50 car mark know that we are sold out. We do limit meals to 1 bag per car. I'm so sorry for any inconvenience, but we are trying our best to cook for as many people as possible. I hope y'all understand that this is our first pandemic, too. I can't wait to get back to business as usual and back to our regular menu and service. Love you all, and wish everyone the happiest and safest Easter possible!

👍❤ 1.3K   233 Comments 41 Shares

Late March | The New Normal

Curbside meals continued this way for weeks, as time seemed to stand still. The routine remained the same: four kitchen personnel cooking as much as they could, seven days a week, while two of us with gloves and masks on placed meals in the back of cars and did contact-free credit card processing through the front window. I dropped by Waters several times, but sales there seemed to be lagging far behind the Bonnell's location.

Sales overall were good enough to support the restaurants, but with tips pouring in, it was time to make a decision about just how to spend that surplus. It was not as simple as handing out tips just to the servers who used to work in the dining room. These tips were intended to help out all of our staff. Everyone was due their final paycheck on Friday for their last week worked before the shutdown. I made sure we let every employee know that they needed to come in person to get their last check. We divided the cash, prorated based on how many hours each person used to work. Most received several hundred bucks in cash in that last-check envelope.

Customers were generous enough with their tips to keep this practice up for the next 2½ months. All former employees of Bonnell's and Waters received supplemental income because of this incredible display of humanity. I was truly humbled and amazed by the generosity of strangers in such dire circumstances. I wanted to give a hug to former employees with each envelope we gave out, but social distancing was becoming routine now, so envelopes were placed on a counter. At least we

could talk to each other from across the room.

I was really starting to miss seeing everyone on a daily basis. The restaurant felt so empty with just the few of us working. No customers inside the building, no kitchen printers furiously buzzing away, no lively, bustling atmosphere. Former employees started coming to the curbside once in a while just to be around other people, hanging out from a distance but still able to talk to each other and even see some of their regular customers through car windows. We all still needed each other. Humanity was searching for camaraderie at this point, and very few places offered the opportunity for any sort of human connection.

The streets were almost completely empty as the town followed "shelter in place" orders. I gave permission slips on the company letterhead to each employee, along with my cell number in case they got pulled over. It just proved that they were "essential employees" and had an excuse to be driving around.

The most common phrase uttered at the curbside: "Thank y'all so much for doing this!" My wife often came up to work the

"Humanity was searching for camaraderie."

Late March

curb as well, usually running the margarita machine as I stuffed meals into cars, one at a time. For the two of us, this brief window of social time with a few employees, getting to see the smiling faces of customers through their car windows, seemed just enough to feel at least a little more normal, if only for a couple of hours. I was just glad we could still be in business!

The traffic at Waters Restaurant died down pretty quickly, and many nights did not see a sellout. The usually lively downtown area now felt eerily empty. We dropped the family four-packs down to two-packs at Waters, then finally decided to unite the two kitchen teams into one force on March 31. With eight people running a single kitchen at Bonnell's, scheduling that included days off now became a possibility. We worked out a more realistic schedule, and transported the two-pack meals downtown right before service time. It saved money overall and gave the kitchen staff much more workable shifts.

Here is a time-lapse video from May 20, showing how 600 people got food using the curbside setup.

April 20 | Right Place, Wrong Time

I almost forgot completely about the plans that we had
formulated for the opening of our fifth restaurant in the Bonnell's
group, Jon's Grille. We had negotiated the lease, my brother and
I had started a beef program with cattle on his family ranch, and
we were on track to get open by the fall of 2020.

One week before the final signature on our commercial lease,
COVID-19 exploded and I had all but forgotten about the deadline
to sign the paperwork when my agent gave me a call. "I know
you're busy, and I think I know the answer, but do you still want
to open this new place, Jon's Grille?" Struggling to keep alive the
four restaurants that we currently had, I knew there was not a
chance in the world of opening another one in 2020. We did not
want to give up entirely on the concept of Jon's Grille, but the
timing was certainly not right, to say the least.

I asked my agent if we could just punt the entire thing down
the road a bit and get an extension on the lease terms that we had
already agreed upon. The landlord was incredibly generous and
accommodating, giving us plenty of time to weather the storm
before signing on the dotted line. We decided to wait until the
fall before revisiting the project but still kept the cattle program
moving along just to keep our options open.

**"I know you're busy, and I think I know the answer,
but do you still want to open the new place, Jon's Grille?"**

"Y'all Stay Home" was the city directive, and for the most part, we did just that.

Early April | Patterns and an Epic Prank

A few weeks into the "new routine," I noticed that our family had fallen into very distinct patterns. I would wake up very early and hit the couch with a laptop, posting the daily menu and sometimes composing an email newsletter to the other restaurants. Before I knew it, lunch would roll around. My 8-year-old

Texas Students Will Repeat Current Grade in 2021

Abbott: Texas Students Will Repeat Current Grade in 2021

Best prank ever!

son Ricky was up before the others, but he would melt off into his iPad before long and play games with his friends before his online school classes started. My 12-year-old daughter Charlotte was the late sleeper. The school still required both kids to maintain some routine of classes for their online learning.

By the time lunch rolled around, we'd often grab something from another local restaurant, then I'd head into work. Melinda, my wife, would usually be in charge of dinner, although some days I grabbed an extra family meal just because it was the easiest thing

to do. The hustle and bustle of sports, activities, parties and gatherings with friends just had to wait on the sidelines for a year. "Y'all Stay Home" was the city directive, and for the most part, we did just that.

I found a meme online one afternoon and was able to pull off the most epic prank on my kids. It featured the governor telling all students that because of in-school classes being canceled, everyone had to repeat their grade the following school year. It looked official enough, and my wife and I decided to give the kids almost 30 minutes before telling them it was all a joke. Best prank ever, especially given the circumstances!

Spring–Early Fall | Staying in Touch

I missed the variety of events and interactions with people that we used to enjoy. The restaurant business is a tremendously social industry — at least it once was. We all craved more personal interactions, but our orders were clear: Shelter in place. I took my son out to the ranch several times just to get out of the house and off the iPad. We visited his grandfather (my dad) on a few occasions, but it was always through a glass window while talking on speakerphone. No hugs, no high-fives, just waving through virus-protecting glass barriers for now.

The family would all go fossil hunting or fishing, any activity we could find that fit the required parameters of being outdoors and socially distant. I began to despise the words "socially distant." I'm a people person, in a people-oriented business, so the socially distant

Visiting my dad, Bill, on speakerphone through glass on March 21.

"No hugs, no high-fives, just waving through virus-protecting glass barriers for now."

lifestyle left me lacking. On the flip side, we had never enjoyed this much family time with each other in our lives. We had no commitments, no meetings, no big dinners that I needed to attend, nothing on the calendar, so every night our family was gathered around the table together. We've never been so close as a family while being so removed from everyone else.

I can't help but wonder what this time will feel like from our kids' perspectives. Will they fondly recall the extended break from school, or will they just remember being bored to death from a lack of friends to play with? Did they get too much family time, or was this the closest we've ever been? How will my wife and I reflect on this crazy time? It was difficult to see where and when this whole thing would end, as each day became a more defined pattern, the future completely ambiguous.

For my son's 9th birthday, we hosted a birthday parade. We stood in our front yard while all of his friends drove by in their cars, screaming out of the windows, standing through the sunroofs, and throwing candy into the yard. Some made hilarious signs or dragged balloons behind them as the slow-rolling birthday parade raucously rolled along our street. I may or may not have fired off a few illegal fireworks left over from Fourth of July, 2019. It was socially distant (grrrrr, those damn words again), kept everyone safe, and still gave my little man a sense of being special, even if just for 10 minutes or so. Best birthday idea ever? Biggest letdown yet? Only time will tell.

My son Ricky's 9th birthday party. Friends paraded by in cars, throwing candy from the windows and sunroofs.

"Brisket prices actually got higher than prime rib."

Spring-Summer | Supply Chain Challenges

Grocery stores were mobbed early in the pandemic, and long lines formed outside them as more customers than ever were cooking from home. The supply chain was in chaos, as our society switched from driving to work and school or making travel plans to just staying put. Simple ingredients that we used to order for the restaurants without a second thought became scarce, or their pricing tripled overnight.

Brisket prices actually got higher than prime rib at one point, and chicken was hard to come by. Ground beef, just the basic stuff, was priced in line with sirloin steak, and we struggled every week to make affordable menus that we could continue offering curbside. Some days, I was OK with losing a little money on the meals, since we could at least shoot for some profit with "extras." At least we were still working and providing some kind of service.

Several of my friends had chosen a different approach with

The line at an area Sam's Club 45 minutes prior to opening.

their restaurants and just closed them temporarily, waiting for a better business climate to rehire and reopen. Some days I really envied that approach, as our rules for operation and supply chain issues got overwhelming at times, but overall I was glad we still maintained some position in the food-service business. It felt like one part business survival mixed with one part community service, but I couldn't imagine just waiting it out, trying to pass the time until better days. I'm too restless to sit still that long.

We entertained that option in our original meeting, just closing until things got better, but I nixed that one quickly. I remember telling the staff that night, "I'm not one to fight often, but if we choose to fight, we're gonna fight like the third monkey in line for Noah's ark right when it starts to drizzle." And fight, we did.

Mid-Spring | Responsibility and Relief

Keeping up the email newsletter became a responsibility that I couldn't take lightly. It even had become a borderline obsession. In times when I felt completely helpless under the circumstances, at least I could do something to help others, something validating, something of worth. When the governor held a press conference, I took notes. When the mayor or county judge needed to give us information, it was an easy and efficient process.

I reached out to Sen. John Cornyn's office, and to his credit and my surprise, I was on the phone with him the next day. Some very encouraging news began to circulate about financial help for restaurants from the federal government, and over the span of quite a few communications, Sen, Cornyn shared details on a plan that he intended to support — what would later become known as the Payroll Protection Program. This was the most encouraging news I had heard since this whole thing started.

In late March, the CARES Act was passed quickly (even before the details had been written) and money was set aside specifically to keep employers from letting workers go. By mid-spring, we received the first round of PPP. This changed everything, not just financially but in spirit as well.

"In times when I felt completely helpless under the circumstances, at least I could do something to help others."

April | Time To Rehire

We had already let the vast majority of our staff go, but PPP funds gave us the opportunity to bring some people back! This was a massive turning point. I convened a meeting of some key staff members whom we wanted to bring back on board and, just like that, we added shifts and saw the return of some of our most tenured employees. It was exciting to have more people around the restaurants, and customers loved getting to see the familiar faces of favorite servers and bartenders working the curb! The kitchen was able to bring in more help as well, and the morale and scheduling improved dramatically. And I didn't have to be the only guy placing bags in back seats anymore!

We even found ways of creating more elaborate meals for special occasions like Easter. We took pre-orders for prime rib meals, finally going back to the more high-end cuisine, if only for a short time. Easter meals were still served chilled with simple heating instructions, and handed off contact-free, but at least we were able to elevate the level of cuisine for a special occasion. Sales were through the roof, as many customers had been craving more of what we earned our reputation cooking for all these years, and we were eager to step up our game again.

"Customers loved getting to see familiar faces."

"COVID-19 just got personal."

April 14 | One of Our Own

On April 14, I learned the tragic news that our Fort Worth restaurant community tragically lost one of our own. Wade Sanders, "The Wine Dude," lost his battle with COVID-19 after a long stretch in the hospital. His family had said goodbye when he left by ambulance, not realizing that it would be the last time they'd ever see him in person. Wade was one of those characters who brought a smile to everyone's face. His knowledge of wine was unsurpassed, but he threw it around jovially, without the slightest bit of pretension. Wade was a fixture at every Food +

We will dearly miss "The Wine Dude."
R.I.P. Wade Sanders.
Photo by Ralph Lauer

Wine fest event I'd ever attended, and had been a friend and colleague for as long as I could remember. COVID-19 just got personal, as this was the first real friend whom I lost to the pandemic. It wasn't just jobs and dollars anymore. He was a father, a husband. A

funeral parade was organized, T-shirts were printed and a seemingly endless stretch of tributes to a life well-lived rolled slowly by Wade's house. Hopefully, his wife and kids, who were sitting in lawn chairs out front, felt the outpouring of love, sympathy, and respect that we all wished to convey from our vehicles. I wish I could say I lost only one friend to COVID-19, but sadly, by the end of the year, my list had grown to 14.

A young man who was a dear friend of mine called me one

April 14

afternoon from his college in Washington State with the tragic news that his mother had passed away from COVID-19 in her home, without warning. His last phone call with her had been the day before, with her complaining of a terrible cough and fever. Just like that, another life snuffed out — a mother, a sister, a friend.

As their family members from around the country tried to gather in Fort Worth, they couldn't find anywhere that would allow them to meet together. I told him, "Screw the rules. Just come meet on the Waters patio with your family. You guys need this time together to mourn, to plan, just to be together. If

anyone gives me grief, I'll pay the damn fine." We ordered pizza and sandwiches from Buffalo Bros down the street, left out some wine and drinks, and gave this poor grieving family their space.

The day came when my wife gave me a speech I'll never forget. "I need you to know that one day, everything will be OK. You have to stop feeling sad once in a while, and realize that this WILL get better, and we WILL be OK. I need you to believe that." I'm usually the eternal optimist in the family (to a fault), but I hadn't felt hope in a long time. As much as I tried to hide it, she knew me too well. The kids caught me crying a few times, but I tried to play it off as best I could manage.

"Space was the one thing we now had plenty of."

April | Closing Downtown Down

The Waters curbside service in downtown Fort Worth eventually slowed down enough that we decided to just go dark there for a while. Luckily, we could still keep those employees on the payroll and have them fill in at Bonnell's for the time being. Rumors began to circulate that there might be a chance of reopening dining rooms soon. With both teams joined together in one location, it almost felt busy at times, even though the dining room wasn't open yet. Staff kept on their masks, maintained proper distancing, and worked at computer stations spaced well apart, since space was the one thing we now had plenty of. I kept pressing the governor's office for information, but they held all details very close to the vest.

Finally, toward the end of April, I got a tip that we had some good news coming soon and I needed to watch the next press conference by Gov. Abbott. My excitement and anticipation were dampened somewhat once the official statement was announced. Texas was ready to gradually reopen restaurants, but only at 25% occupancy for starters. That rate of occupancy certainly wasn't going to cover our bills, so we decided to just stay the curbside course with our consolidated teams. Everything in the restaurant business revolves around total sales. We start with the overall number, then shoot for a percentage of those sales to go toward food expenses, a percentage to spend on labor and, hopefully, use the remainder to cover fixed costs like rent and utilities. At 25%, there was not enough left after fixed costs to even think about opening the doors.

Downtown business slowed to the point that Waters was closed.

41

April 13 | Social Media to the Rescue

In April, only a couple of weeks into the "Y'all Stay Home" orders, I got a call from the early morning crew at Bonnell's saying that we had been robbed. I couldn't believe that in the middle of this crazy pandemic, someone would actually burglarize a restaurant! By the time I got dressed and headed into work, my manager had already reviewed the footage on our security cameras. We all watched, jaws dropped, as two individuals just pulled right up, parked in the handicapped spot (a nice touch, I thought) and brazenly walked right up to the back door of Bonnell's Restaurant. They looked around for a while, smoking cigarettes and talking, then made off with four very large ice chests, one axe (used for the wood pile), and one shovel.

They sped away, only to return 20 minutes later and proceed to steal one of our stainless steel commercial smokers, detaching the hard-wired 230v electrical cord. It weighed close to 300 pounds, costs $10,000 new, and these two (one male, one female) had the nerve to just roll it out to their pickup, using the handicapped ramp (makes more sense now), and lift it into the back! I called the police to make a report and quickly published the pictures and video to my

Facebook page.

Social media ran with this story faster than anything I've ever witnessed. It amassed more than 1,700 social media shares by the next morning. Being under lockdown gave everyone plenty of time and motivation to help solve the case. Local news picked up the story and leads began pouring into my inbox faster than I could read them.

One friend described the exact details of the truck, including the year, model, and several after-market details that would make this vehicle a one-of-a-kind. Another friend believed he had seen the same couple at 7-Eleven getting chased out by the manager just a couple of miles away. I needed gas anyway, so I headed over to that 7-Eleven and talked briefly to the manager, describing what happened and showing him their pictures. He knew exactly who they were, saying that he'd given their license plate to a 911 operator when they shoplifted at the store. He told me they lived just a few blocks away in the adjacent neighborhood.

I drove around for less than 5 minutes before seeing the

unique truck and the couple both inside. I quickly took a pic of their license plate and called the police as I sped away. Maybe it wasn't the smartest move to pursue the suspects myself, but emotions got the best of me and I just couldn't help myself. Once I gave the police the picture of the truck, it only took one day to put the driver behind bars. He had multiple other offenses and it appears this one tacked onto the others might just earn him several years in the state prison. The woman turned up a few months later, was charged with three felony counts and is currently waiting to see her legal outcome.

I laughed out loud when the Fort Worth Police Department called to tell me that they had already apprehended the thief,

and I was truly in awe of the quick work by our amateur Facebook crime fighters, as well as our local law enforcement professionals. Three days after his arrest, I received another call from the detective on the case and she asked if I was currently at Bonnell's to receive "a special delivery." They arrived in under 5 minutes with my smoker, fully intact! My electrician came by to reinstall the wiring and in under 10 minutes, the unit was up and running again. It was even still full of wood!

The police had received a phone call from someone asking, "Hey, like, uh, if I know where that famous smoker thing is, can I just show you where it's at, aaaaand like, I'd be OK, like not in trouble?"

Posted this note just in case they returned.

"Social media ran with this story faster than anything I've ever witnessed. It amassed more than 1,700 social media shares by the next morning."

April 13th, the smoker comes home!

May | A Virtual Helping Hand

Jon Bonnell
May 15, 2020

Another legendary spot in Ft Worth needs some help, y'all! Been downtown since 1931! If you're around, grab some BBQ. Outstanding chopped sandwich! Support Local! please share

Jonah Horton, Lisa Grubbs and 434 others   40 Comments 286 Shares

I had been using Facebook so often that my online presence grew exponentially. Friends, followers, fans, whatever title Facebook gave them, my overall online game became an extremely powerful tool. There were days when I despised social media for the way it allowed otherwise civil people to jump down each other's throats, but overall it was still an important tool. Through many different forms of communication — email, various social media platforms, news channels, etc. — it became apparent that many local mom & pop establishments were not faring too well.

Closures were happening right and left, and a feeling of helplessness hung over restaurant owners. Rents were still due, utilities still had to be paid, yet sales were still plummeting. When I saw another FB user put out a call for help, not for their own establishment but for someone else in need, it seemed like the simplest gesture in the world to just tap on the "share" button. Bigger influencers and food bloggers joined in, and the call for help went virtually viral. The struggling restaurant quickly had more business than it could handle, simply because the online community decided to actively pitch in.

One local reporter wrote in his column: "I'm glad Bonnell's is doing well, but that line is long and there are plenty of others who need help as well. Y'all spread it around." Seeing how powerful that one little online "share" turned out to be sparked a new idea. Instead of just promoting our menu, I could use our new online presence to help promote everyone. We were selling out every night, so why not leverage the online influence to benefit others with our platform?

We began to promote other establishments, spread the news of their menu offerings and specials, and help encourage the public to "Eat Local" and remind them why. We even started a list of every independent restaurant in the city. Every time a user posted something like, "Where should I eat tonight?" or "What great local spots do y'all recommend?" I had the list ready to post as an answer. Some people even used it like a bingo card, trying to get through the entire list before the pandemic was over. The sense of community in Fort Worth is very strong, and the response to these calls for help was immense. This technique helped steer some traffic to those who needed it quickly, and assisted those who desperately wanted to help but didn't know how.

"Many local mom & pop establishments were not faring as well as others."

July 19

Please keep supporting your favorite Local Ft Worth Independent Restaurants! Thank you for all of the support, Ft Worth! Here's your checklist of places to keep in business. Lemme know if I missed someone. Please share!

360 Smoke Shack, 817 Pizza, Ampersand Coffee, Angelos, Arizola's , Aventino's, Avoca, Babe's, BBQ Ranch, Bearded Lady, Bella West, Bella Pasta Pizza, Benitos, Ben's Triple B, Berry Street Ice House, Black Cat Pizza, Black Coffee, Black Rooster, Bluebonnet Bakery, Bombay Grill, Bonnell's, Boopah's Bagels, Branch & Bird, Brewed, Brix BBQ, Buffalo Bros, Byblos, Cafe Bella, Cafe Istanbul, Cafe Republic, Cajun Market, Cane Roso, Cannon Chinese, Cardona, Carpenter's Café, Carshon's Deli, Cat City Grill, Cattleman's Steakhouse, Chadra, Charlie's Hamburgers, Chicken Salad Chick, Clay Pigeon, Coco Shrimp, Craftwork Coffee, Crude Craft Coffee, Cousin's BBQ, Curley's Frozen Custard, Dayne's Craft BBQ, Del Campo Empanadas, Derek Allen's BBQ, Dive Burger Bar, Don Taco, Dos Molinas, Doughboy's Donuts, Drew's Place, Dusty Biscuit Beignets, Dutch's Burgers, Edelweiss , El Rancho Grande, Ellerbes, Enchiladas Ole, Esparanza's, Feastivities, Fixe, Fixture, Fortuna, Four Sisters, Flying Carpet , Fratelli Pizza, Freds, Fuego Burger, Funky Picnic,

Supporting local restaurants

Funky Town Donuts, Gallagaskins, Gepetto's Pizza Truck, Ginger Brown's, Grace, Great Harvest Bread Co, Great Outdoors, Greek House, Grounds & Gold, Gypsy Scoops, Gyro Kabobs, H3 Ranch, Happy Bowl (Thai), Heim BBQ, Hookers Grill, Horseshoe Hill, Hot Box Biscuits, Hurley House, Italy Pasta Pizza, Japanese Palace, Jazz Café, Jesus BBQ, Joe T's, Juice Junkies, Jube's Smokehouse, Kincaid's, King's Kitchen, King Tut, La Onda, La Playa Maya, La Rueda, La Tortilandia, Las Pericas, Lettuce Cook, Le's Wok, Lilly's Bistro, Little Germany, Little Lilly Sushi, Little Red Wasp, Local Foods Kitchen, Loft 22 Cakes, Los Asederos, Los Vaqueros, Lucile's,

Lucky Bee, Lunchbox, Magnolia Motor Lounge, Maharaja, Mamma's Pizza, Mancuso's, Margi's, Mariachi's, Meli's Taqueria, Melt Ice Cream, Meyer & Sage, Mi Cocula, Michael's, Milano's, Montgomery Street Café, Nana's Kitchen, Neighbor's House Grocery, Nonna Tata, Old Neighborhood Grill, Ole South Pancake House, Our Place Restaurant, Pacific Table, Pack a pocket, Paco's, Panther City BBQ, Paris Coffee Shop, Paris on 7th, Park Hill Café, Parton's Pizza, Pearl Snap Kolaches, Perrotti's Pizza, Piatello, Piola, Pouring Glory, Press Café, Prima's Italian, Provender Hall, Pulido's, Qana Café, Race Street Coffee, Railhead, Reata, Righteous Foods, Rio Mambo, River Bend, Rodeo Goat, Rogers Roundhouse, Rufus Bar & Grill, Salsa Limon, Sammie's BBQ, Samson's, Sausage Shop, Shaw's Burgers, Shinjuko Station, Sikhay, Simply Fondue, Smokeaholics, Smokeys BBQ, Smokestack 1948, St Emilion, Star Café, Sushi Tao, Swiss Pastry Shop, Szechuan, Taco's Ernesto, Taste Community, Tastebud's Eatery, Thai Select, Thai Terrace, Thailicious, The Meat Board, The Original, The Tavern, Tie Thai, Tinie's, Tokyo Café, Tommy's, Tributary, Tuk Tuk Thai, Tulips, Vallartas, Vickery Café, Wabi Sabi Sushi, Wasabi, Waters, West Side Café, Wicked Butcher, Wild Acre, Winslow's , Wishbone N Flint, Wizard's Burgers, Wooden Spoon, Woodshed, Yeschf Cajun, Yogi's, Yoko's Donuts, Yucatan Taco, Zeke's, Zoli's

Mid-May | It's in My Blood

"After all, I did have a fever for a little while back in February."

In mid-May, I was still asking my brother (the medical expert) questions about COVID-19 almost daily. I had never been tested for it but was extremely concerned for myself, my family, my employees, and my customers. We were being as safe as we could be, using gloves, masks, sanitizer, everything recommended to help prevent the spread of this virus. I kept wondering if there might be a chance that I already had it but didn't know it. After all, I did have a fever for a little while back in February.

Finally, he recommended I take a blood test called the IgG and wrote me a prescription. Off to the lab I went for a quick blood draw, and just like that, the next day I received word that I was positive for the long-term antibodies of COVID-19! I had already had it and never knew; same for my wife! It turns out we both likely got this virus in February in New Orleans

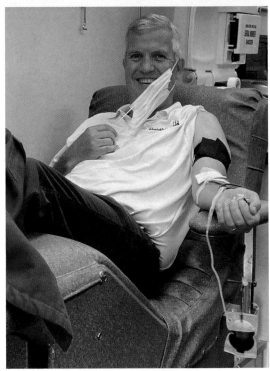

I was able to donate 10 units of plasma and 2 units of whole blood before getting my vaccine. For some reason, my antibodies stayed high for well over a year!

during Mardi Gras, back before we had even heard the word "pandemic." Nobody was worried in February, but in hindsight, it looks like we should have been.

The feeling was liberating, knowing that I had those antibodies in my blood and was basically "safe" to be around people. I still wore a mask and practiced all safety protocols, but I certainly felt a tremendous peace of mind knowing that our household was biologically very protected. I'm pretty sure our kids had developed antibodies by that time as well, but we decided not to stick a needle in them to find out for sure. I found a plasma center nearby and asked about donations, knowing that I had some lifesaving antibodies in my bloodstream, and they directed me on how to proceed. The first visit took almost three hours of paperwork, blood testing, a lengthy questionnaire, and even a physical, but finally I was hooked up to the machine and it began to extract my plasma. It took roughly an hour, very much like donating blood, but near the end of the process, after the plasma had been run through an extracting machine, my red blood cells were then injected back into my arm.

I began to donate these antibodies through plasma roughly once a week. If convalescent plasma could help save lives, I was all-in. I also received an almost desperate plea to help get more blood donations into the regular blood bank for the Fort Worth area. Just like every other part of our economic system, the blood donations had all but dried up during this time. We began scheduling bloodmobile drives at Bonnell's, since we had a somewhat high profile and certainly a highly visible place to encourage people to donate the gift of life. I pulled the big Bonnell's grill into the parking lot, cracked open a cold beer and offered anyone willing to donate blood a bacon cheeseburger to-go just for being good citizens.

Our blood drive filled up every available time slot in the first 30 minutes of going live online! The next time, we scheduled two bloodmobiles and filled those slots just as easily. Once again, the people of this great community were more than willing to help out their fellow citizens — something that Fort Worth has been doing really well for a very long time.

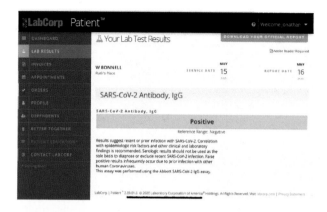

A blood drive for my cousin, George Howard Porter, was arranged when his surgery was postponed due to lack of O blood supply.

"For the time being, we continued stuffing bags in back seats at the curbside."

Early June | **Opening Up!**

At the very beginning of May, Gov. Abbott finally began to discuss what we were all desperate to hear: his plans to safely reopen our industry and our city. I eagerly took notes and tried to pick out every important detail as he spoke. Phase 1 was just the beginning, where restaurants were given the opportunity to open at a 25% overall capacity, with 6 feet of spacing required between tables (or physical barriers such as plexiglass), sanitizer stations throughout, and many other "bells and whistles" attached. No silverware, glasses, menus, or anything other than single-use items could be placed on tables.

This would be very different than a standard fine dining experience, but at least we were moving toward opening rather than closing! As I ran the numbers, I couldn't find any way possible to justify opening with only 25% of the tables available to customers, so for the time being, we continued stuffing bags in back seats at the curbside. Inside dining would just have to wait. Fortunately, we still had enough sales to make the business run, and we were able to start hiring again!

On May 19, Gov. Abbott scheduled another press conference, and once again, I found myself typing tedious notes. I hadn't been this studious since college! I felt a certain sense of obligation to make sure that every restaurant on my list got accurate and up-to-date information. Phase 2 increased the dining room capacity to 50%, just enough for our team to begin putting plans together for a "Grand Reopening"!

Many customers wondered why we didn't just open the doors and start right away, but hiring back staff, ordering product, prepping, and "COVID-izing" the interior was going to take some time. Waters was first, with an opening date of June 9. We ordered everything we needed and brought back as many staff as we could afford, and just like that, Waters was back to shucking oysters and delivering seafood towers to patio tables. In-person dining came back to life! All physical menus were changed to a QR Code system, tables were left bare and sanitized between seatings, and servers learned a completely new type of service, wearing masks and following an entirely new set of safety procedures. For the first time in months, we were back in the fine dining game, and the feeling was both liberating and exhilarating!

Bonnell's continued to serve hundreds of people from the curbside every night, seven days a week. The idea of opening up the restaurant dining room, too, felt daunting, to say the least, but we worked for weeks on a plan. How could we continue to feed Fort Worth from the curb while opening the dining room and bar at the same time? Waters had already returned to indoor and outdoor dining, but the situation at Bonnell's was a bit more complicated.

My team racked our brains for a solution, then Catering Chef James Pallett finally came up with a workable solution.

James was in charge of the majority of production and was the single most valuable member of our team, so his opinion weighed quite heavily on these decisions. Our final answer was to reduce our workweek to five days, operating both inside and curbside from Tuesday through Saturday, with two separate teams in the kitchen producing the two very different menus. New Executive Chef Charles Youts would head up the in-house team, while James continued with the high-volume family meals. Our opening date was set for June 19, and some key staff were brought back on board to help breathe life back into the restaurant. For weeks, we did as many deep-cleaning and touch-up projects as possible, knowing now that we had some PPP funds that could be used for employees. It was not as simple as just flipping a switch, but turning the restaurant back to the "on" position was happening, finally!

Video of
Waters reopening

Video of
Bonnell's reopening

June 11 | **Protests Hit Close to Home**

After 86 days of being closed to diners, Waters Restaurant finally opened the interior and patio spaces for fine dining on June 9. For the first time in a long time, guests and staff were smiling again. The sun was shining, the freshest seafood was glistening atop mounds of crushed ice, Champagne bottles were popping, and all seemed to be looking up in Sundance Square. COVID-19 was by no means over, but at least we had the first inkling that businesses were beginning to climb out of the deep, dark hole we'd been wallowing in for months.

On June 11, everything once again changed gears. If I never hear the word "pivot" again, that would be just fine by me! Protest marches had been happening for weeks all over the city, from West 7th Street to Main Street. Black Lives Matter and other groups organized, marched and made their voices heard. For the most part, Fort Worth was still peaceful, with no major violent clashes, riots, burning or looting.

I called one of my close friends from high school, an African American buddy of many years, and asked if he might join me one evening in one of the marches. He almost fell off his couch laughing, stating, "Man, *I* wasn't even going to join those guys, but if one of my white friends is going to invite me to a protest, Brother, I am IN!" It gave me an excuse to see an old friend, catch up all afternoon and be part of history, rather than just watching it walk by that evening. We enjoyed great conversation all afternoon, ranging from the pandemic and marches to our families and even old friends and classmates. It felt great just to

Jon Bonnell is with Terrence Butler.
June 5, 2020 · ⊘

I don't care much for politics, but I do care about people. This is my friend, and he's my brother is Christ. His Life Matters!

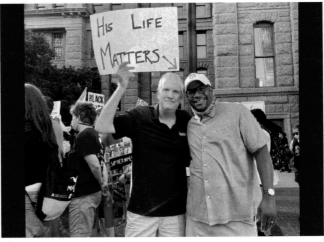

👍❤️😲 2K   182 Comments 58 Shares

be out of the house or the workplace for a change.

Some of our conversations were difficult and awkward, and we definitely didn't agree on everything we talked about, but then again we didn't have the same experiences growing up. I will never know what it truly felt like to live in his skin, nor he in mine. It didn't make us like each other any less, or lose any amount of respect for each other, but difficult discussions like this have long been overdue in so much of our nation. I'm so glad we had the chance to share this time together. Honestly, given the heat and the chaos, we didn't even march all that far before veering off and heading back to Waters to continue our conversation.

"We're hurting, too! We've been closed over 80 days, and we just got back in business this week."

We made a great social media post together and had thousands of feedback hits from friends, some of whom we had forgotten we even knew, almost unanimously supportive. Some were just checking in to say hello. We set up a series of multiracial group talks over the next few months with friends and acquaintances, and asked for varying opinions to be shared. No-holding-back kinds of talks — just honest statements about how you feel and why. It felt much more productive for us to gather groups like this together, than for just two old pals to hang out.

Suddenly, on the evening of June 11, my phone began to blow up with text messages from other restaurant owners and security officers from Sundance Square in downtown Fort Worth. Another group of protestors had formed, somewhat of a splinter group from the earlier marchers, and these guys were beginning to take protesting to another level. This group was entering restaurants in large numbers, and situations had become extremely tense. I watched an impassioned speech from one of their leaders on the steps of our courthouse, just a few blocks away from Waters, and it sounded very ominous — to say the least — for the days to come. I wasn't in the mood to fight with anyone, but it looked like some kind of fight was about to come looking for us. Here's what was said:

"We gotta quit goin' down to West 7th street. They don't give a fuck about West 7th street. We're gonna fuck up what they care about, which is downtown Ft Worth! From this day forward,

we're gonna hit every fuckin' restaurant in downtown. I'm puttin' y'all on notice. From this day forward, every fuckin' restaurant in downtown is gonna see our goddamned faces, and we ain't goin' nowhere motherfucker!

I hadn't been sleeping well in general since March, but the night of June 11 was worse than usual. I knew they were coming, and I knew to expect potentially aggressive behavior. I'd seen videos of other restaurants that they had entered and it wasn't pretty. The police department promised to station an officer inside every restaurant, but they also warned us to lock our doors when the marchers came by. Under NO circumstances were we to let any of the protesters enter our doors.

The idea of welcoming customers back to a full-service dining room with open arms, celebrating our grand reopening, then locking the doors with everyone inside while possibly ill-intentioned marchers filed by seemed like a tremendously dangerous plan. I can deal with an individual person in almost any situation, but crowds are very different, and I was scared. This was a "wear your brown pants" kind of situation. Customers came in, dressed to the nines, and I faked my best smile for the beginning of the night, hiding my overwhelming sense of anxiety and anticipation.

As darkness began to fall, I kept watching out the window toward the courthouse, until finally I could see the march beginning just a few blocks up Main Street. I locked the side

June 11

door and positioned myself by our front door on Main and turned the key, explaining to customers nearby that we were just taking some precautions and they needn't worry. As the group passed by, the language may have been a little salty, a few middle fingers were thrown my way, and few bumps were made on the glass, but all in all they marched on peacefully and my stress level and blood pressure dropped tremendously.

Customers quietly thanked us for providing a modest level of security, and it felt nice to finally get back to the business at hand. About 10 minutes later, my heart rate skyrocketed as an employee whispered quietly and strategically into my right ear while I was chatting with some guests, "Chef, they're coming up to the patio. You better get out there."

The protestors had a permit to use the streets and sidewalks and had every right to demonstrate outside of our patio, but I had foolishly not even thought about a plan for our outdoor diners. And there were plenty of outdoor diners on this gorgeous

Making peace with protesters and handing out water.
It was June in Texas, and it was hot!

June evening! To describe this as a tense scene would be quite an understatement, as fancy towers of seafood, chilled wine, and Champagne adorned the tables. The chants as the group headed up the block were not subtle by any means, and the protesters weren't going to turn around at the corner. They marched directly up to our patio railing, over a hundred strong, with bullhorns in hand. Tensions were high. As one of their leaders began to shout, I recognized him as the man from the YouTube video of the courthouse speech that I had watched the night before, threatening all of downtown. I stayed back at first, just observing from the corner of our bar, terrified as to how this was all going down, frozen like a deer in the headlights.

"When we come up like this and talk to y'all, does it make you uncomfortable?! Good, cause it fuckin' should make y'all uncomfortable! Y'all need to be uncomfortable!!!" Then, suddenly, he spotted me by the bar. "Hey, looks like we got ourselves a community leader right back there. That's Jon Bonnell. Come on up here Jon and tell me something. I need you to tell the mayor something for me!"

This is a video from NBC, which had a camera crew embedded in the crowd.

10:05 79°

"What would you like me to tell the mayor?" I responded, knowing that I was committed to seeing this through, with no chance of just observing by the bar any longer.

"Can I ask you something?" I said to him. "What makes you think I'm not on your side? Did you know that I've been out there marching with y'all? Your life matters to me, his life matters to me, and her life matters to me" I said, pointing at each of the people at his side. "I'm not against y'all. When I saw that video of George Floyd dying, I cried. I'm not here to fight with y'all. But we're hurting, too! We've been closed over 80 days, and we just got back in business this week. I'm not against y'all, and I have no reason to fight with ya. We just want to be in business, too."

I motioned for him to come up the steps to the rail, and to his credit he walked right up. I gave him a quick hug and the crowd actually gave us a little applause. After a few fist bumps, they respectfully marched on to the next block. Many of the customers gave them some applause as well, showing respect for the way everyone had handled the situation with a modicum of calm and understanding. Tensions had been defused for now, and a great sense of peace finally came over me. I needed a drink! Luckily, I was still just a few steps from the bar, and I swear the first cap I twisted had the finest taste of any beer I'd ever experienced in my life! Whew. That could have gone in a completely different direction, but luckily, cooler heads prevailed.

A few minutes later, the Fort Worth Police Department

Kudos from Patrons and Protestors

Josh Terra Richards
Jon Bonnell We were there eating last night. You're a class act. Standing at the front door at the protestors peacefully walked by. I know it's been a rough run for restaurants. We pray for you and your team often.

Megan Lanning
Love this!! We were there eating at Water's tonight supporting you! I'm proud of them! And you! Thank you for the great meal and standing up for what is right. 🖤

Jacqueline Bender
I particpated in the march last night and when we came upon your restaurant, signs and support, the whole vibe changed. I felt hope. You and your team demonstrated understanding and support and it was powerful.

46w   Care   Reply   43 👍❤️😮

Mounted Patrol rode by on horseback, and the customers gave them a little applause as well. They had been patrolling extended hours for days, rarely if ever engaging the protesters, mainly just controlling the areas and trying to keep everyone safe. There were a few incidents around the city that escalated, but not here, not tonight, not in Sundance Square. I didn't realize until my phone began pinging constantly in my pocket that the local NBC affiliate had a camera crew embedded in the crowd and captured the entire thing for the evening news. For the first time in weeks, I slept like a baby that night.

Knowing that the same scene was likely to unfold again on the night of June 13, I came up with an idea. I've always preferred having a strategic plan over reacting defensively in difficult situations. What kept coming to my mind was how unified we all seemed to be when the video of George Floyd first came out. It was horrific, and everyone I knew was shocked and saddened. How could we get back on that page where we all felt pretty much the same, rather than screaming at each other in the streets and on the social media outlets? How did we end up in such different corners so quickly? I came up with what I felt were the sentiments that we could completely agree upon, and wrote them down in words that I chose myself. I wanted the protesters to know that I understood why they were marching, and wanted to show empathy, just not in the exact language that some of them were using. I decided to make signs to show support for the things that I believed we agreed on universally, rather than highlight any differences that we might have.

"GEORGE FLOYD DID NOT DESERVE TO DIE"

"BLACK LIVES MATTER TO US, TOO"

"RACISM IS NEVER OK, NEITHER IS SILENCE"

I even tried to show a little humor with one of them to help ease tensions, kind of a mixture between a dad joke and chef humor.

"THE ONLY BLACK THING I HATE ARE JELLY BEANS! THOSE ARE NASTY"

On the evening of the 13th, customers on the patio were told about what was likely to happen as the protestors approached, but this time we knew what to expect. Several customers even asked if they could join in and hold the signs themselves. As the protesters marched around the corner, there was a palpable sense of aggression and energy brewing. As soon as they came to our railing, we held up the signs high, and the crowd erupted in applause. I told them to help themselves to the cooler full of water bottles that I had iced down on the sidewalk for them. "It's hot out tonight. Y'all be careful and drink plenty of water." One protester even asked if she could come back and apply for a job, since her restaurant owner had fired her when he found out that she had been protesting. I wasn't trying to make any kind of political statement with our actions, just trying to keep the peace and show some empathy. We needed more understanding and less conflict, especially after the year we'd been having. I got some hate mail and harsh criticism from both political extremes, so maybe I was

Jon Bonnell

Jun 2, 2020 · 🌐

Proud of my city in so many ways. Well done, Ft Worth. Police Chief and protestors having a simple and honest moment of humanity. I think we all have much more in common than we have to fight about. Please see the good in each other more than the differences. Praying for more of these moments to come. Hundreds arrived and stayed, ready to be taken to jail. Instead they reached an understanding and all left without incident. No arrests on Monday. 🙏

on the right track.

After a few days, the overall number of protesters and their enthusiasm reduced considerably and it felt like we could go back to the regular business at hand. It was time to go back to masks, 6 feet of spacing, and 50% occupancy, but at least we were open again — indoors and out!

> **"All restaurant owners and operators were now in the mask enforcement' business as well."**

Late June | One Step Forward, Two Steps Back

June of 2020 felt like the biggest roller coaster of emotions for many reasons in the restaurant business. We made it through reopening at 50% (Phases 2 and 3 of the governor's plan), and even got promoted up to 75% at one point. We made it through the protests. Then, more of "the rules" began to emerge. Yes, we had all been wearing masks and gloves for quite some time, but the rules of the game in late June were just beginning to be spelled out, and specific legal changes were going into effect faster than many of us could keep up with. The email group probably got tired of seeing my information, as the number of details kept emerging and changing so rapidly, but I kept everyone informed as best I could manage.

The summer gave a little, and the summer took back, but we all kept our heads down and kept weathering the storm in the restaurant industry. In addition to being in the hospitality business, all restaurant owners and operators were now in the "mask enforcement" business as well. We didn't ask for this job title, but it became very apparent that mask policy was going to fall onto our plates during this time, and severe penalties for non-compliance were possibly going to be levied on anyone who chose not to play by the rules.

The online scene (social media postings, etc.) began to get vicious as arguments on both sides of the mask requirement were now fully focused on restaurant and retail establishments. If a business owner refused to require masks or enforce social distancing, they risked losing their liquor license. Operators who strictly complied with mask mandates faced an onslaught of ridicule and punitive food-site scoring reviews from those who demanded individual freedom and personal choice.

One evening, a customer refused a free mask at Waters Restaurant and threatened violence against the employee who offered a mask to him, prompting one of the most ridiculous, yet entertaining, online debacles I've ever been a part of. When the customer was asked to leave the establishment for his actions, he and his wife both began a formal "online war" for the next three days. Nonstop social media posts, phone calls to the restaurant with lewd and threatening messages to anyone who answered, texts to employees — a full battery of assault was waged against Waters.

With a very limited audience, I assumed they would finally just fizzle out over a few days, and I was more than happy to just let the argument fall upon deaf ears for a while. Then one morning as I was posting our daily curbside menu, I found that this customer had changed gears in his online assault and began posting on the Waters Restaurant Facebook page, rather than just his own. I debated whether to engage with this behavior for quite some time before finally just hitting the "share" button.

Once his message went out to my vast online audience, the chatter went truly viral. I literally could not keep up with the comment section as the online response poured in from every corner of the internet. Friends of mine laughed and said that their evening entertainment for several days involved opening a nice bottle of wine and just scrolling and reading comments out loud from this post — almost like a new social media drinking game, our own little online reality show.

I wish that had been the only online incident that reared its ugly head, but alas, several patrons decided to make their greatest stand against the mask rule by berating restaurant employees. We didn't ask for this responsibility, but the burden of enforcement had landed squarely in our laps. Several places decided not to enforce the rules quite as strictly, and they faced online retribution in different ways. Some establishments had their liquor licenses revoked altogether. Being open during the pandemic got more challenging but also strangely more entertaining by the day.

June 24

In the morning, Tarrant County Judge Glen Whitely will be announcing a mandatory mask rule for all of Tarrant County. This will include all business personnel, employees, and patrons alike. He will likely give specific details as to when they can be removed by guests, etc. in the morning. Crowds of over 100 must also wear them, etc. I believe the press conference is scheduled for 9:30 and the rule will go into effect immediately. I'd plan on getting masks on everyone first thing tomorrow. I'll keep y'all posted.
Jon

June 24

The TABC has indicated that they will be the likely enforcement group that will be checking establishments for violations including maximum occupancy violations, spacing violations, and mask requirements. Just a heads up, that customers and other establishments can now call the TABC on us for these types of offenses. Please stay safe, y'all. The last thing we need is more restaurant and bar closures.

Sent from Chef Bonnell's iPad

June 25
The mask requirement will officially go into effect tomorrow night (Friday) at 6:00pm. It officially runs through August 3rd at 6:00am. Masks required for all employees and guests. Ordered by Tarrant County Judge Glen Whitley. The Chamber of Commerce does have a free supply of masks available if anyone needs them.

June 25
Here's the official order from Judge Whitley. The Governor today, also said that the reopening of Texas is officially paused for now. We are still in phase 3 and do not have to back up, but further openings and lessening of restrictions will be paused for now.

June 25
This is a fantastic new website put together by a group called the Ft Worth Strike Force. The Mayor, along with many business leaders like John Goff have put this resource together to have one central hub that small businesses can go to for information. I was honored to be part of this group, and they have done some great work. It is very simple to use, very informative, and I strongly recommend everyone take advantage of this new resource. Every grant and loan you can apply for is listed here, along with lots of other types of assistance that can be extremely useful. Check it out!

https://fwtxnow.com

June 26
Governor Abbott is about to announce that restaurants are backing up to 50% max occupancy, and bars are shutting down. Effective at noon today. I'll let y'all know if I hear any more details. Sorry for the bad news.

Heated Response to Mask Mandate

I never threatened violence against anyone in your organization. You are being lied to. I would never, ever threaten violence to anyone off of my own property. That is how you get arrested. So your claim is 100% wrong and says alot about you as an owner of a business. You further attacking me personally says it all. I now know why your staff are the way they are, it is accepted and pushed by you as their boss. All shit rolls down hill as I was told by my first mentor. Meaning....the owner, ceo, president sets the tone for the company/business. How the employees behave is the tell all to who the owner is and what they are about. You could have ended this by apologizing for your staffs action and how our visit went. The end. And in fact I was actually thinking about deleting my post....and this morning you jumped in and challenged me personally so here we are...running again. And now you relit it by bringing to your own page. Your staff started this and now you are adding insult to injury and the turd rolling down hill is getting bigger. Let dance Jon, I know this one well.

21h

You have made a business enemy in Fort Worth. Shit just got real. I have spent way too miluch money with you to ever be treated like this. ▓▓▓▓ and i loved you and your rest. Game on!

No where in your response have you apologized for affending a loyal client that has spent factually 100s of thousands of dollars and benn one of your biggest fans and supporters. I will find an attorney to file suit regardless of cost and nothig short of your managers job, the expo that physically challenged me an appology will suffice. Your staff is enforcing an unenforcible guideline. You will lose this. I am positive if this.

I have now tagged and shared this to multiple friends and peers. That means tens of thousands potentially now know your business is unfriendly to patriots. Your continued silence is going to cost you.

Last I thought, I don't live in communist China. We were just kicked out of a restaurant for not wearing a mask to the bathroom. A restaurant full of people not wearing masks...I guess the virus only is contagious upon movement...fuck you Jon Bonnell!

Latest Rules include Masks, Groups of 10, Social Distancing

October 13

Hello everyone,

Hope y'all are getting through everything ok. I attended a meeting with Judge Glenn Whitley last night, then had a good call with Mayor Price just to get some clarification on the rules for restaurants and bars going forward. Here is the basic deal for now, of course always subject to change.

Restaurants:

Capacity is maxed at 75% of your Certificate of Occupancy. That only means customers, employees are not counted in that number. Patios are not limited by the C.O.

Masks are required for anyone who is standing. Employees must wear them at all times.

Social distancing of 6 feet between tables is still required.

Eating and drinking may only be done while seated.

Maximum table guest count of 10 people.

Bars: (opening Wednesday)

Bars must stop serving alcohol at 11:00pm. If a bar has changed their permit to "restaurant status", this does not apply, however they must still sell food at the 50% level to maintain this status.

Capacity is limited to 50% of the Certificate of Occupancy. The only means customers, employees not included in that number. Patios are not limited by the C.O.

Masks are required for anyone working, and any patron who is standing, even if dancing.

Eating and drinking is permitted for seated patrons only.

Maximum table guest count of 6 people.

Tables are still subject to 6 feet of spacing for social distancing.

ENFORCEMENT OF THESE RULES:

The enforcement of these rules can and will be done by all of the following agencies:

TABC: This is the most powerful group, since they have the power to remove a liquor license from a bar or restaurant. There are very few TABC agents, but they wield a lot of power. Bars who make no effort towards social distancing, masks requirements, or capacity limits will likely be visited by the TABC and face serious consequences. Social media is playing a large part in this. As videos of crowded places get shared around, political figures are increasingly under pressure to send out TABC officers.

FWPD, Fire, Code Compliance & Sheriff's Dept: Officers are allowed and encouraged to enforce capacity violations, mask violations, and distancing violations. Capacity (75% for restaurants, 50% for bars) will be a no-tolerance violation for the establishment. Mask violations can result in citations being given to the establishment and/or the individual who is in violation. Spacing violations (6 foot rule) is likely to be slightly more lenient as long as the establishment is not in flagrant violation. Patrons who are not wearing masks, drinking while standing, drinking while on the dance floor, etc. are all subject to citation, as is the establishment who allows it to happen.

Let's hope this is just a step in the right direction of opening fully for all of us. If we see increases in hospitalizations, or flagrant violations, we are all subject to moving backwards rather than forwards in this opening process. Stay safe everyone, and let's keep moving in the right direction! If you know anyone else who needs to be on this email list, just send me their address and I'll add it.

Hang in there,

Jon

Fort Worth Food + Wine Foundation offered grants for displaced workers. View the video with QR Code scan below.

In addition to the newfound responsibility of deciphering and explaining the pandemic rules, there emerged another, much more rewarding aspect of running the email newsletter. As grants and loans became available to businesses, I really enjoyed the chance to share those opportunities with my colleagues. The PPP loans were the first to give a lifeline to a dying industry, but many other resources also became available.

A group of Fort Worth business leaders, led by John Goff and Mayor Betsy Price, formed a committee called the Fort Worth Strike Force and organized an initiative that helped provide direct grants for the independent restaurants of Fort Worth. This utilized federal dollars provided by the CARES Act, and took some very smart and dedicated business minds to distribute properly and stay within all the proper guidelines. Texas Christian University business students even volunteered their services to help any small business get their paperwork and financial data in perfect order to ensure some of these grants came through.

I was in awe of the community support behind these initiatives — everyone from business leaders and college students to CPAs all volunteering to help keep the mom & pop restaurants alive during these times. The Fort Worth Food + Wine Festival even awarded over $115,000 in grants to help restaurant industry personnel who were in financial crisis.

Fall 2020 | Is the End in Sight?

By fall, many signs were pointing toward a possible end to this terrible pandemic, although we were not out of the woods by any stretch of the imagination. The biggest news around my house was the return of in-person school! My kids (third grade and eighth grade) had not been to school since they let out for spring break back in March. Sure, there were online classes over Zoom, but social interaction and the entire school experience and usual activities had been missing for quite some time.

There were plenty of new rules and procedures, but everyone was getting pretty used to the mask and distance thing by this point. My daughter had her 13th birthday party in August, inviting her friends to a local park. Each girl had a designated hula hoop and blanket to sit on, properly spaced apart, and an individual meal to prevent contact. They sat around in the shade, just telling stories and catching up. Some of the girls had not been around other kids for months, and even though it was a socially distant event, I could tell they had truly missed human interaction with their peers. A group of eighth-grade boys just mysteriously appeared and threw a football around the park as well, one of the most amazing coincidences!

As the holiday season rolled around, restaurants like mine had no idea what to expect in terms of business and sales. The season is usually jam-packed with in-house private parties, catered events, and large family gatherings. It is typically the highest sales-producing time of the year. Because families were encouraged NOT to gather in large groups, our takeout business from the curbside actually increased. Normally, we would sell anywhere from 65 to 100 complete turkey dinner meals for families to pick up and heat at home for Thanksgiving. In 2020, we sold 265 full turkey dinners from the curb!

While business inside the restaurant was starting to pick up, it was still capped at 50% of overall capacity. However, to-go orders were skyrocketing. With regular curbside family packs, holiday special orders, and 50% sales inside the restaurant, for the first time in a long time, my kitchen was at pretty much maximum output capacity. The typical holiday parties and gatherings were not on the calendar, so this new format was starting to contribute some real and much needed financial stability to our bottom line.

Not quite the kind of birthday party I remember as a kid.

"In 2020, we went through hell, but in 2021, hell froze over."

February 2021 | Snowmageddon

After the winter holidays, the next opportunity for big sales typically comes in February for Valentine's Day. As luck would have it, Valentine's fell on a Sunday in 2021, so that meant the possibility of a very busy weekend, plus a good bonus day of sales, since we are normally closed on Sundays. Our Bonnell's and Waters locations were poised for business and fully stocked with very nice products for the special weekend when the unthinkable happened.

On Saturday, Feb. 13, weather predictions for all of Texas called for a massive snowstorm (by Texas standards, anyway). It became obvious that our Valentine's Day dinner service was going to be canceled. To help retrieve some of the losses, I posted a very attractive price on lobster bisque and lobster tails, all available at the regular curbside location. By the end of the day, we sold 120 tails, and over 9 gallons of lobster bisque, all through car windows in to-go containers, then we braced for the storm that was beginning to bear down on the Lone Star State. Mayor Price said it best, "In 2020, we went through hell, but in 2021, hell froze over."

The storms took away any chance for service on Sunday, as ice and snow covered the roadways in a city with extremely limited equipment to clear any of it away. We get the occasional snow in Texas, but not enough to validate the expenditure of a full fleet of snowplows. My kids were predictably excited about making a snowman, instigating a raucous snowball fight, and even getting in a little sledding on the local golf course. Snow days were

Melinda and the kids were always helping, even during Snowmageddon.

always the best days when I was a kid.

The mood quickly changed that evening when our power went out. As it turned out, much of Texas lost power, and the timeline for it returning was questionable. A fun winter dusting of snow quickly escalated into a major disaster for the entire state. An enormous pileup of cars, trucks and 18-wheelers on the interstate caused multiple casualties, one of them a relative of one of my employees. It felt as if 2021 was just trying to outdo 2020 by this point, and once again things got personal.

Three out of our four restaurants were closed for the week, while the largest of our sports bars, Buffalo Bros in Sundance

Square downtown, struggled to keep the fires burning. The power never went out there, but all of the major food suppliers grounded their delivery trucks due to hazardous road conditions. Will-call was open, so I became a delivery driver pretty much full time for the week, stocking as much food as I could fit into our catering van on each trip.

Some employees were able to make the drive in, but we were still a little short-staffed most of the week. Only two restaurants in the entire downtown area were operating, so our production was at the maximum capacity possible, surpassing even our highest sales from Super Bowl Sunday. Many customers were lined up on the sidewalk for hours waiting for a table, since the maximum seating indoors was still capped at 50% during this time.

The fire marshal removed our patio heaters outside, citing that the sidewalk was public space, and we didn't have permission to place them anywhere other than our actual property line. Once people were seated inside, many brought phone or laptop chargers and used every available outlet to charge up, catch up on communications, warm up and drink up, often all at the same time. My family and our pets moved to my brother-in-law's house for a few days as well, since the temperatures inside our house hovered in the 30s. One night cuddled around the fireplace was enough for us. Water pipes were bursting in houses and buildings all over town, and a boil-water notification was issued for much of the city when water mains began to burst as well.

Once again, my email newsletter was buzzing with the latest information about which parts of the city could use their water, and which restaurants were allowed to be open. Many new rules and regulations went into effect when the quality of the city water

Jon Bonnell
February 13 · 🌐

In anticipation of the snow tomorrow, Bonnell's will be offering lobster tails and smoked lobster bisque at the curbside tonight (Saturday) as extras (regular dinner is fried chicken).
8-10 oz Maine lobster tails for $26 each (cleaned and split, ready to cook), and pints of smoked lobster bisque are $16 each. Combo kit, one of each $40!

couldn't be verified for a few days. The Presbyterian Night Shelter (one of the largest homeless shelters around) lost power in their main facility, and their kitchen was rendered unusable. With 600 residents still living there, they sent out a desperate call for help to feed the guests one evening. With a quick phone call and one email, we were able to put a team of volunteers together and produce over 1,300 sandwiches. We delivered them just as the power was coming back on.

Snowmageddon: Making 1,300 Sandwiches, Boil Water Notices

February 16

The Presbyterian Night Shelter needs some meals and they have no power, no kitchen, but of course tons of people. I need a group of volunteers to help put sandwiches together today at Bonnell's at 4:00. If you can make it, please let me know. I don't want to use FB, as that could get out of hand pretty quickly. It's just assembling 1,000 sandwiches so not a huge skill set required. Shouldn't take all that long. Please lemme know!

Thanks,
Jon

February 16

Hello all,

Thanks for everyone who volunteered with me today! We cranked out over 1,300 sandwiches for the shelter in under an hour, wow!

So, now for the somewhat good news. The Covid 19 numbers and hospitalization rates have dropped enough, for enough days, etc that we are officially back to 75% capacity. There is still the 6 foot rule, it's not a rule that has a specific enforcement protocol. There is a big time problem if you are over total capacity limits, but very little can actually be enforced on the spacing requirements. I'm not suggesting that you ignore this rule, but when Code Enforcement comes by, they are looking primarily for overall capacity and enforcement of mask rules. Those are the violations that get the attention right now. I hope you are all staying warm and safe. Let's get the power back on, the water back on, and get back to cooking!

Take care,
Jon

February 19

Good Mornin' fellow restaurant folks. Hopefully we get above freezing today and thaw everything out! Just a couple of things today. Bud Kennedy shared this map with the exact "boil water" area map that I wanted to pass on. If you are in the boil zone, the restaurant cannot open. Reasons include hand washing, ice machine, Coca Cola lines, iced tea, dish washing, etc. I wish there was an easy fix, but there is not until the water comes clean through the pipes. From what I hear, you will need to burn off all old ice as well and start with new ice production after this as well as clearing all lines of water that might have been contaminated.

On another note, the Comptroller has extended our tax deadline (monthly sales and liquor) for this month. What is usually due on the 20th, we now have until the end of the month to pay, basically.

Hope this helps,
Jon

February 19

If your establishment is in one of the "boil water" areas, the city is allowing you to open, but certain safety measures are being required. These are unique times, and the city is trying to offer us a lifeline. See below for ways to open if you choose to.

Mr. Bonnell,

Brandon Bennett asked me to send you this information, which is also being sent to other restaurants.

Business owners, operators and employees:

Yesterday, the City of Fort Worth Water Department extended the boil water notice for the western and northern areas of the city. (https://www.fortworthtexas. gov/news/2021/02/Water-Boil-Notice) The boil water notice is in effect until all water is tested and safe to drink.

Historically, food establishments, under a boiled water order, have not been allowed to operate as this is considered an imminent public health hazard. Water coming from the faucet cannot be guaranteed to be free of hazardous bacteria that may increase the risk of illness.

Given the unprecedented nature of the recent events, food establishments under the current boil water order may operate, but only if temporary guidance for food service and handling are met.

This guidance is available at the link below and it must be followed if you choose to open for food service:

https://dshs.texas.gov/foodestablishments/pdf/ GuidanceDocs/Guidance-for-RTE-under-Boil-Order.pdf

With best wishes for your health and safety,

February 19

The "boil water" notice for North Ft Worth has been lifted. West is still in effect, hopefully over soon as well.

February 21

Boil Water Requirement is over for all of Fort Worth! https://www.fortworthtexas.gov/news/2021/02/Water-Boil-Notice

Sent from Chef Bonnell's iPhone

Sledding

March 2021 | The Final Call From the Governor

On March 1, I got a good tip that Gov. Abbott's next press conference was going to be a very big deal and that I needed to watch and take proper notes. The conference was filmed inside an independent restaurant, which gave me great hope for the upcoming announcement. After a very short introduction and a few stats about COVID-19 case numbers and vaccine reports, the big news dropped like a bag of hammers! "As of next Wednesday, all restrictions for businesses in Texas are officially lifted." I never imagined I could tear up from a press conference, but this was the best news I'd heard in such a long time! All restrictions, mask mandates, capacity limits — the entire kit and caboodle was done! After 358 days, the rules and restrictions governing restaurants were finally over. I could hardly wait to send out this set of emails!

The pandemic was by no means over, not by a long shot, but this signified the beginning of the end for all of us. As vaccines became more readily available and "survivors" of COVID-19 felt more and more comfortable heading back out, restaurants all across the city began to fill up once again. We still kept our masks on, and we encouraged patrons to do the same, but the opening up of Texas felt liberating.

As I'd walk by the tables in Waters or Bonnell's, inevitably every other party would say something like, "We've been home

 Jason Perkins is with **Jon Bonnell** and **3 others**.
Jun 9, 2020 ·

So glad Waters is open again and we can hang with our friends.

for an entire year, just waiting until we felt safe enough to go out. This is the first place we came back to." These words fueled my soul, as it felt like things were actually going to be OK, finally. My wife was right all along!

Finally, Good News

Hello ALL!

This is great news for us today! Governor Abbott just announced today that ALL restrictions and mask mandates in Texas will be over starting NEXT WEDNESDAY! Here are a few of the bullet points from his speech:

Due to an abundance of PPE, plenty of Covid-19 testing (over 100,000 daily now), advanced medicines and treatments, and most importantly VACCINES, Texas is ready to open up completely. 5.7 million vaccines have already been administered (over 216,000 in a single day). By Wednesday, 7 million shots will have been administered. Over half of the senior citizens in Texas have been vaccinated already, and by the end of the month it is projected that every senior who wants one, will have been offered one. He also estimates that every single Texan will be offered a vaccine who wants one in just a few months total. With over 10 million recovered and vaccinated, coupled with only a 9% positive testing rate today, he believes it's just time to open fully.

Covid-19 is by no means gone, but with safe practices and improved medicines and vaccines, Texas will now reopen fully.

Businesses are fully allowed to have any policy that they want. You may keep the restrictions and/or mask policy, but you do not have to. No citizen in TX will be punished by any law enforcement for not wearing a mask. The State will rescind the previous mandate (from October) that we are currently under.

In addition to rescinding the previous Mandate, the Governor will also restrict any individual County Judge from imposing any capacity restrictions or mask mandates unless their County Hospitalization Rate goes above 15% for 7 consecutive days.

We are all completely free to set our own policies moving forward. Congrats, everyone! We're turning the corner! I'm not crying, you're crying!!!

March 2

Immediately following the Governor's press conference, Tarrant County Judge Glenn Whitley dropped the mask mandate for the entire county immediately. There is no need to wait until next Wednesday. The mask mandate in Tarrant County is over. You may choose to enforce any policy you want. Beginning next Wednesday, the capacity and 6 foot spacing requirements will no longer be in effect. Again, choose any policy moving forward that you see fit for your business.

March 2

As most of you have already seen and experienced, the mask/no mask policy is absolutely blowing up online right now. Some customers are trying to put together a list of "safe" restaurants that still require masks, while others are ready to go maskless with reckless abandon. It is up to each business to set their own policy and enforce their own rules from now on. There is no longer a mandate to back us up. I hope we can all try to support each other as much as possible, no matter what choices each establishment chooses for their place of business. I plan to use the following language on my doors:

WE ENCOURAGE ALL PATRONS TO CONTINUE SAFE PRACTICES CONCERNING COVID-19 THAT HAVE BEEN SO SUCCESSFUL THIS PAST YEAR, AND WE PLEDGE TO CONTINUE WITH THOSE STANDARDS FOR OUR EMPLOYEES AND STAFF.

I know how hard this is going to be. We are encouraging customers to wear masks, but not requiring it. I'm sure we will get plenty of grief from both sides on this one. I wish you all the best in this truly difficult time, but also congratulate all of you for getting to this (hopefully) final stretch in the pandemic. May this truly be the beginning of the end!

Cheers to better days ahead!

Jon

Good Morning Quarantinis! Hello Frontage Roadsters! Some of the Bonnell's and Waters Curbside Meals

Brisket

BBQ Shrimp

Chicken Parmigiana

Chicken Pot Pie

Shrimp boil

From March 21, 2020–March 10, 2021, a total of 82,636 people were served dinner from the curbside at Bonnell's Restaurant and Waters Restaurant. Only four cooks prepared those meals from each location. The curbside program at Bonnell's still continues to this day, with no plans to end the service in the near future.

The Memes That Kept Us Going and Laughing

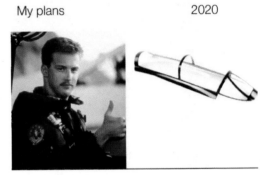

2020
IS STILL
BETTER
THAN MY
FIRST
MARRIAGE

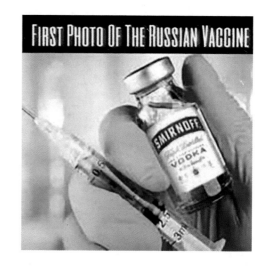

FIRST PHOTO OF THE RUSSIAN VACCINE

Kenny Rogers dippin out in the middle of an apocalypse is the most... "know when to fold 'em"... thing ever

2021

SURPRISE, SURPRISE

On Monday, May 3, my Calendar app had me scheduled for a private dinner at Waters Restaurant, Sundance Square. I had been notified that Mayor Betsy Price had rented out the entire restaurant privately to have one last hoorah before her official retirement from office in June. I pulled up to the restaurant about 6 o'clock, assuming we would go over the last-minute details and setup, but quickly realized when I walked in the door that something was definitely askew. The entire place was already full, and as I looked around, I saw mostly other restaurant owners, chefs, managers, even some of my own staff

members from other locations. When I glanced over and saw my dad, I knew for sure that this was NOT just a party for Mayor Price. Her office had arranged for a surprise party in recognition of all the work I had been putting in over the past year to help the restaurant community, and for the first time in my life, I was pretty much left speechless. I had been sending out emails to the entire independent restaurant community for over a year, and they were all there to say thank you. I'm not afraid to admit that this night made me tear up a little. I'm glad my wife, Melinda, and both of our kids were there to be part of the evening as well.

CLOSED FOR PRIVATE EVENT

CELEBRATING CHEF BONNELL

Mayor Price's speech honoring Jon Bonnell